WITNESS TO WAR

THE US CIVIL WAR

KELLY ROBERTS

What can we learn from the people who witnessed war?

CHERITON
CHILDREN'S BOOKS

Published in 2025 by **Cheriton Children's Books**
1 Bank Drive West, Shrewsbury, Shropshire, SY3 9DJ, UK

First Edition

Author: Kelly Roberts
Designer: Paul Myerscough
Editor: Sarah Eason
Proofreader: Katie Dicker

Picture credits: Cover: Shutterstock/Everett Collection; Inside: p1: Shutterstock/Everett Collection, p3: Shutterstock/Karyl Miller, p5: Shutterstock/Jeff Kinsey, p6: Shutterstock/Everett Collection, p7: Shutterstock/Everett Collection, p8: Shutterstock/I. Pilon, p9: Shutterstock/Everett Collection, p10: Shutterstock/Everett Collection, p12: Shutterstock/Everett Collection, p13b: Shutterstock/Everett Collection, p13t: U.S. Naval Historical Center, p14: Shutterstock/Everett Collection, p15: Shutterstock/Karyl Miller, p17b: Shutterstock/Everett Collection, p17t: Brooklyn Museum/Eastman Johnson, p18b: Shutterstock/Everett Collection, p18t: Shutterstock/Everett Collection, p20: Library of Congress, p21: Shutterstock/Everett Collection, p21b: Shutterstock/Everett Collection, p22: Shutterstock/Everett Collection, p23: Shutterstock/Everett Collection, p25: Shutterstock/Everett Collection, p26: Shutterstock/Everett Collection, p27: Shutterstock/Everett Collection, p28: Shutterstock/Everett Collection, p29: Wikimedia Commons, p30: Shutterstock/Everett Collection, p31: Library of Congress/Currier & Ives, p32: Shutterstock/Everett Collection, p33: Shutterstock/Everett Collection, p34: Shutterstock/James Kirkikis, p35: Shutterstock/Kamira, p36: Shutterstock/Everett Collection, p37: Wikimedia CommonsBurns Archive, p38: Shutterstock/Everett Collection, p39: Shutterstock/Everett Collection, p40: Shutterstock/Everett Collection, p41: Shutterstock/Everett Collection, p42: Shutterstock/Everett Collection, p43b: Shutterstock/Bill Perry, p43t: Shutterstock/Brandon Bourdages.

Printed in China

CONTENTS

CHAPTER 1

THE CIVIL WAR

For as long as humans have lived together in groups, there have been wars. People go to war for many reasons—fighting, for example, over religion, natural **resources**, or ideas about how a government should be run. Many wars are fought between two or more countries. When two sides within the same country fight against each other, it is called civil war. Those involved in the American Civil War would witness the devastation of war—and in doing so, become a witness to history. In this book we will look at some of their stories and their words as witnesses to war.

Starting the War

The Civil War began in 1861 when a group of Southern states voted to **secede**, or separate, from the United States of America. They believed that President Abraham Lincoln intended to end slavery. Together, these Southern states formed the Confederate States of America.

Over the next four years, war raged between the Confederate and Union armies. It is now believed that more than 600,000 Americans may have died in the Civil War. Many were killed in battle, but far more died as a result of disease and poor medical treatment. Even today, the war remains the bloodiest in US history.

WITNESSES TO WAR

In this book we will hear the words of witnesses to the war: the people who experienced the conflict firsthand. We'll discover what impact the war had on them and what we can learn from their accounts. In each case, read the source and the notes, then try to answer the questions.

The Civil War had such an impact on Americans that to this day, key battles are reenacted.

The Fight for Families

When we think about war, we often think of the soldiers who fight. However, many of those most affected are the families left behind. This was certainly the case during the Civil War. Women and children on both sides of the conflict faced many hardships, but they did whatever they could to help the war effort and support their fathers, brothers, husbands, and sons on the battlefield.

Understanding PRIMARY SOURCES

The eyewitness accounts in this book are primary sources. A primary source provides direct information about a subject. Examples of primary sources include diaries and letters. Along with the eyewitness accounts in the book, we will also look at some other primary sources, such as photos and drawings, which provide important information about war and the experience of war.

The American Civil War

The Civil War was fought between the Confederate army of the South and the Union army of the North. Though many issues of the time divided Southern and Northern states, one of the most important was the issue of slavery. Nearly 4 million Black people were enslaved in the United States before the start of the war. Slave labor was an important part of the South's **economy**. However, many people, especially those in the Northern states, felt that slavery was wrong and should not be allowed.

A Different Way of Life

Before the Civil War, life in Northern states was very different from life in the South. The economy in the North was based more on industry and manufacturing. The Southern economy, in contrast, focused on **agriculture**, or farming. Northerners and Southerners also held some very different political ideas.

Living in the South

Plantations—large crop-growing farms—were at the heart of the Southern economy. The warm weather and fertile soil in the South created perfect conditions for growing important cash crops, such as cotton and tobacco. Many Southern families, especially those with smaller farms, did not own any enslaved people at all. However, large plantations depended on slave labor; by 1860, there were nearly as many Black people in the South as whites. Some of these Blacks were free, but most were enslaved people, who were bought and sold, and worked unpaid. Transporting goods through the South, which had few large cities and few railroads, was difficult. For that reason, most goods were transported by river or by sea.

Plantation owners used unpaid enslaved people to carry out backbreaking tasks such as picking cotton.

This group of Black men built a section of railroad for the Union army.

Life in the North

The climate, or weather, in the Northern states was not suited to large plantations. However, the region did have many natural resources, such as coal. Because of this, industry and the manufacturing of goods began to play a larger role in the economy. Factories were built, and towns grew into large urban centers. By 1860, one-quarter of all Northerners lived in large cities.

Northerners often had professional careers in business, engineering, and medicine. Children in the North were also more likely to go to school than those in the South. There was little need for slave labor in the North, and immigrants from Europe did much of the lower-paid work. But mining companies and railroad companies often hired enslaved people from the South to do heavy manual labor.

The Path to War

At the start of the Civil War, the United States had been an independent country for less than 100 years. Following independence from Britain, the US government was designed to ensure that each **citizen** was represented fairly. The number of **representatives** each state has in the House of Representatives is based on its population, and each state has two representatives in the Senate. After independence, the country continued to expand by claiming and adding new areas of land, or territories.

A Growing Fear

As more territories became US states in the 1800s, people feared that either those who supported slavery or those who opposed it would gain too much power in the government. Before 1820, there were equal numbers of slave states, in which slavery was legal, and free states, where it was not. To try and maintain this balance, the Missouri **Compromise** of 1820 allowed Missouri to enter the United States as a slave state if Maine was allowed to enter as a free state; this helped calm the issue for a while.

PRIMARY SOURCE

Selling Enslaved People

This advertisement was placed in a newspaper in 1885. It describes the public auction, or sale, of "five negroes"—enslaved people were widely referred to as "negroes." The wording of the sale describes the enslaved people as if they were trucks or tools for sale, rather than people. How do you feel when you read this advertisement? What does it tell us about the way many Southerners viewed enslaved people?

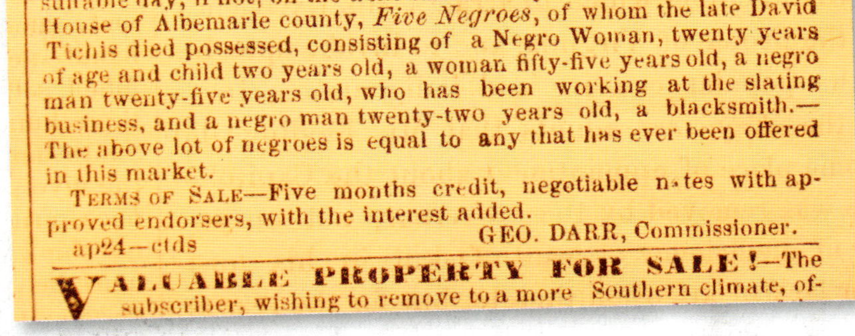

To Messrs. Rove & Co. ap14

PUBLIC SALE OF NEGROES.—Under the authority of a decree of the Circuit Court of Albemarle county, pronouced in the case of Michie's administrator and others, on the 8th day of October, 1855, I will offer for sale, at public auction, on MONDAY, the 5th day of May next, being Albemarle Court day, if a suitable day, if not, on the next suitable day thereafter, at the Court House of Albemarle county, *Five Negroes*, of whom the late David Tichis died possessed, consisting of a Negro Woman, twenty years of age and child two years old, a woman fifty-five years old, a negro man twenty-five years old, who has been working at the slating business, and a negro man twenty-two years old, a blacksmith.—The above lot of negroes is equal to any that has ever been offered in this market.

TERMS OF SALE—Five months credit, negotiable notes with approved endorsers, with the interest added.

ap24—ctds GEO. DARR, Commissioner.

VALUABLE PROPERTY FOR SALE!—The subscriber, wishing to remove to a more Southern climate, of-

WITNESS TO WAR

A Mississippi planter named Richard Thompson Archer wrote about the right of Southerners to defend their "right" to own enslaved people:

"The South is invaded. It is time for all patriots to be united, to be under military organization, to be advancing to the conflict determined to live or die in defense of the God given right to own the African."

Why do you think Archer speaks about a "God given right to own the African."?

What purpose may it have served Southerners to believe they had a right given by God to own Black people?

Conflict in Kansas

The balance of free states and slave states largely held until 1854, when the Kansas-Nebraska Act repealed, or canceled, the Missouri Compromise. The Act allowed settlers of the new territories of Kansas and Nebraska to decide by vote whether slavery would be legal. Many people were angry, and violence erupted in the Kansas Territory between those who favored slavery and those who were against it. The violent conflicts, which took place over several years, are often called "Bleeding Kansas."

This woman is waiting outside an area that held enslaved people about to be auctioned.

The First Shots

In November 1860, Abraham Lincoln was elected as the US president. Lincoln and his **political party**, the Republicans, opposed slavery and its expansion into new US territories. Lincoln's victory was the last straw for many Southerners.

Forming the Confederate

Just over a month after Abraham Lincoln won the 1860 presidential election, South Carolina voted to secede from the United States. Before Lincoln was inaugurated and took office in March 1861, six more states—Texas, Florida, Alabama, Mississippi, Georgia, and Louisiana—had broken away. Together with South Carolina, the seven states formed the Confederate States of America.

Lincoln took office as the sixteenth president in 1861, and one who was in firm opposition to slavery.

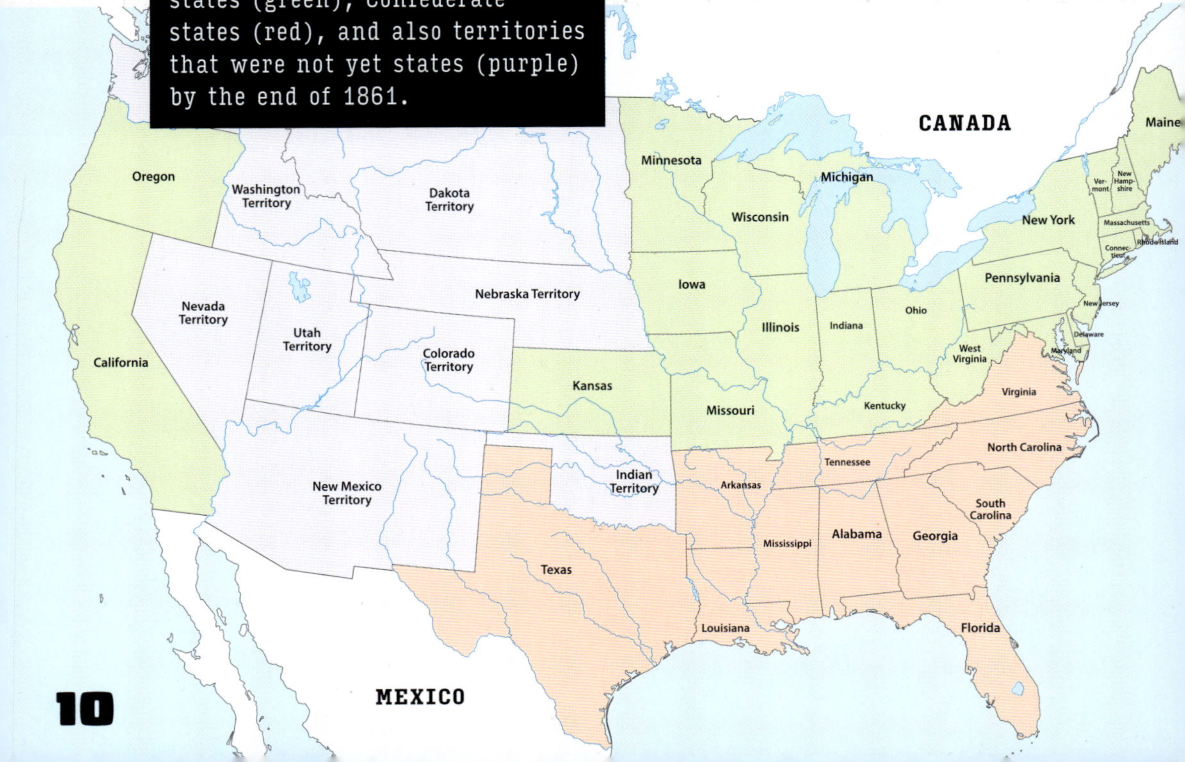

This map shows America's Union states (green), Confederate states (red), and also territories that were not yet states (purple) by the end of 1861.

Trying to Save the Union

In February 1861, a meeting called the Peace Conference of 1861 was held in Washington, D.C. The goal of the meeting was to preserve the Union and reach a compromise on the slavery issue. The meeting, however, was unsuccessful, and the compromises suggested made neither side happy.

No Going Back

By April 1861, tensions were rising between the Union and the newly formed Confederacy, as the Confederate States were also known. On April 12, Union ships attempted to resupply Union troops at Fort Sumter, in Charleston Harbor, South Carolina. Confederate forces fired on the Union troops, who eventually surrendered. Though the Battle of Fort Sumter did not result in any **casualties**, it is considered the start of the Civil War. After three days of fighting, on April 15, Abraham Lincoln called for 75,000 volunteers to join the Union army. Within a month, four more states—Virginia, Arkansas, Tennessee, and North Carolina—had seceded and joined the Confederacy.

WITNESS TO WAR

Stephen D. Lee was a lieutenant general in the Confederate army. He witnessed the Battle of Fort Sumter. This is an extract from his account:

"The firing of the mortar woke the echoes from every nook and corner of the harbor... that shot was a sound of alarm that brought every soldier in the harbor to his feet, and every man, woman, and child in the city of Charleston from their beds ... A thrill went through the whole city ... No one thought of going home; unused as their ears were to the appalling sounds, or the vivid flashes from the batteries; they stood for hours fascinated with horror."

Mortar are guns that fire explosive shells.

What do you think it must have been like to witness the sounds of weapons being fired in your home city?

How do you think these sounds made ordinary people feel?

CHAPTER 2

FIGHTING THE WAR

Many people consider the Civil War to be the first modern war, because of the roles that industry, transportation, and telecommunications played in the widespread conflict.

Many Different Weapons

Civil War soldiers used many different types of weapons on the battlefield. These included knives, swords, and **bayonets**, which are rifles with swords or knives attached to the ends. They also used many types of firearms, such as **muskets**, which needed to be reloaded after each shot. One type—named rifled muskets—used a grooved barrel that caused the bullet to spin as it left the barrel, which helped improve the accuracy of each shot. As the war went on, repeating firearms became more common. These guns, such as the Spencer rifles and Henry rifles, could fire several shots before being reloaded.

PRIMARY SOURCE

Cannon Power

Cannons were also very important during the Civil War. **Artillery**, such as the 6-pounder gun, the 12-pounder Howitzer, and the 1857 model 12-pounder—commonly called the "Napoleon"—were used to fire at enemies, both those in the open battlefield and those behind fortifications. The names referred to the size of the shots fired. Each cannon was a heavy piece of equipment often pulled by horses. This photograph shows a Black soldier appointed by the Union army to guard cannons.

Cannons were also fired at the enemy from nearby ships, such as the *Wissahickon*.

A Fight at Sea and in the Air

Naval weapons also played a role during the war. After the battle between two **ironclad ships**, the USS *Virginia* and the USS *Monitor* on March 9, 1862, ships cased in iron or steel would replace the widely used wooden ships. Airplanes would not be developed for another 40 years, but Civil War forces found another way to use the skies. Hot-air balloons were sent up, primarily by the Union, to gather information about battle sites and the movement of enemy troops. Some could even send messages by **telegraph** to the ground.

Escaping War

Some enslaved people saw the growing chaos of war as an opportunity to escape slavery in the South and flee north.

This article in the "Harper's Weekly" magazine, published in 1863, shows a runaway enslaved person named Gordon who joined the Union army. His back is covered with scars from whippings.

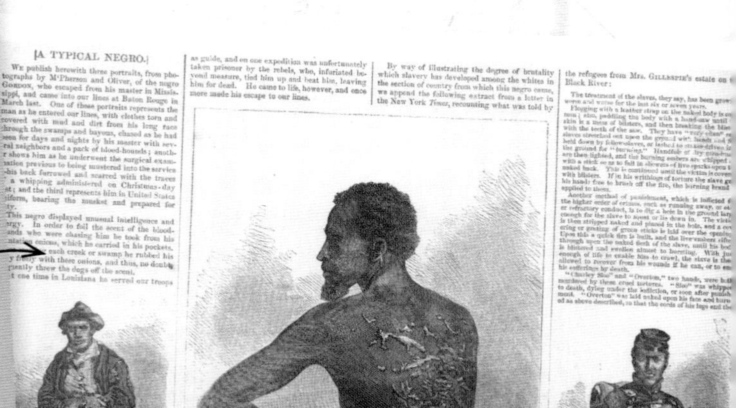

[A TYPICAL NEGRO.]

We publish herewith three portraits, from photographs by M'Pherson and Oliver, of the negro Gordon, who escaped from his master in Mississippi, and came into our lines at Baton Rouge in March last. One of these portraits represents the man as he entered our lines, with clothes torn and covered with mud and dirt from his long race through the swamps and bayous, chased as he had been for days and nights by his master with several neighbors and a pack of blood-hounds; another shows him as he underwent the surgical examination previous to being mustered into the service —his back furrowed and scarred with the traces of a whipping administered on Christmas-day last; and the third represents him in United States uniform, bearing the musket and prepared for duty.

This negro displayed unusual intelligence and energy. In order to foil the scent of the blood-hounds who were chasing him he took from his plantation onions, which he carried in his pockets. After each creek or swamp he rubbed his body freely with these onions, and thus, no doubt, frequently threw the dogs off the scent.

At one time in Louisiana he served our troops as guide, and on one expedition was unfortunately taken prisoner by the rebels, who, infuriated beyond measure, tied him up and beat him, leaving him for dead. He came to life, however, and once more made his escape to our lines.

By way of illustrating the degree of brutality which slavery has developed among the whites in the section of country from which this negro came, we append the following extract from a letter in the New York *Times*, recounting what was told by the refugees from Mrs. Gillespie's estate on the Black River:

The treatment of the slaves, they say, has been growing worse and worse for the last six or seven years. Flogging with a leather strap on the naked body is common; also, paddling the body with a hand-saw until the skin is a mass of blisters, and then breaking the blisters with the teeth of the saw. They have "very often" seen slaves stretched out upon the ground with hands and feet held down by fellow-slaves, or lashed to stakes driven in the ground for "*burning*." Handfuls of dry corn-husks are then lighted, and the burning embers are whipped off with a stick so as to fall in showers of live sparks upon the naked back. This is continued until the victim is covered with blisters. If in his writhings of torture the slave gets his hands free to brush off the fire, the burning brand is applied to them.

Another method of punishment, which is inflicted for the higher order of crimes, such as running away, or other refractory conduct, is to dig a hole in the ground large enough for the slave to squat or lie down in. The victim is then stripped naked and placed in the hole, and a covering or grating of green sticks is laid over the opening. Upon this a quick fire is built, and the live embers sifted through upon the naked flesh of the slave, until his body is blistered and swollen almost to bursting. With just enough of life to enable him to crawl, the slave is then allowed to recover from his wounds if he can, or to end his sufferings by death.

"Charley Sloo" and "Overton," two hands, were both murdered by these cruel tortures. "Sloo" was whipped to death, dying under the infliction, or soon after punishment. "Overton" was laid naked upon his face and burned as above described, so that the cords of his legs and the

ON AS HE ENTERED OUR LINES.

GORDON UNDER MEDICAL INSPECTION.

GORDON IN HIS UNIFORM AS A U. S. SOLDIER.

Women and War

At the time of the Civil War, women did not yet have the right to vote in state or national elections, but many were strongminded enough to form their own opinions about political matters, which could be very different from the views of their husbands.

Harriet Beecher Stowe was one woman who took a strong stand against slavery. She wrote a book titled "Uncle Tom's Cabin," which encouraged people to oppose slavery. This poster was for an 1881 theater production of her book.

Brother Against Brother

The Civil War is often called the war in which "brother fought against brother." While the country was divided over the issues of slavery and the rights of states, many families were divided as well.

Family Fights

In the Civil War era, just as today, families did not always agree on important issues. One family member's loyalty might be to the United States, while another's was to their home state, even when that state decided to secede. Parents might believe that owning enslaved people was their right and necessary for their economic survival, while the writings of **abolitionists** might have convinced their daughter or son that slavery was wrong and should be banned.

Families Torn

During the Civil War, political disagreements tore some families apart. Many fathers, sons, and husbands left their homes to fight in the war—even though the rest of their family did not support their decision. For example, Brutus Clay was a member of the Kentucky House of Representatives who supported the Union. Later in the war he served in Congress in Washington, D.C. However, in 1861, his son Ezekiel Field Clay left home in the middle of the night to join the Confederate army.

The brutality of the war was seen not only in battle, but also in the fights within families.

WITNESS TO WAR

Captain D.P. Conyngham was an officer in the Union army during the war. He witnessed firsthand the terrible toll the war took on families, when a fellow Union soldier, named Driscoll, accidentally shot and killed his own son, who was in the Confederate army, in the Battle at Malvern Hill in 1862. This extract describes the moment when the father realized he had accidentally shot his son:

"Driscoll turned him over on his back. He opened his eyes for a moment, and faintly murmured 'Father,' and closed them forever. I will forever recollect the frantic grief of Driscoll; it was harrowing to witness. He was his son, who had gone South before the war."

Driscoll was overcome by grief. Later in the battle he charged into gunfire and was killed.

Harrowing means extremely upsetting.

What effect do you think witnessing this terrible scene would have had on Conyngham?

CHAPTER 3

WOMEN AND THE WAR

The Civil War had a huge effect on family life. As men went off to war, women were forced to take on new roles at home to ensure their families' survival. Some women had the skills necessary to do so, while others were unprepared for the harsh realities of war.

Women's Work

In most families at the time of the Civil War, both in the North and in the South, the men were the primary breadwinners. This meant that they were the ones who worked outside the home to earn money, or that they did much of the manual labor on the family farm. The older sons in a family also worked and often contributed much of their earnings to their family. Most women did not work outside the home. Instead, they took care of the children and ran the family household, which included work such as cooking and cleaning.

Working for Survival

When the Civil War began, husbands and older sons began leaving home by the thousands to go off to battle. This left many families without any source of income or way to run their farm. Women throughout the North and South had to take on new responsibilities, many of which they were neither trained nor prepared for. Young girls and women at the time were expected to be refined and cultured, but for the most part, had not been taught the many important skills necessary for daily survival.

A New World of Work

Now, some took on their husbands' roles in running businesses. Many began running their family farms, performing difficult physical tasks such as plowing fields and harvesting crops. For women used to hard labor, generally those from poorer families, this new work and responsibility was less of a challenge. However, for many middle-class women—particularly those in the South who were left to run plantations and manage enslaved people—life was very different. Yet, most of these women found the strength to do what was needed to make sure life continued.

With men away fighting and women struggling to keep plantations going, some enslaved people saw the opportunity to escape. This famous painting titled *A Ride for Liberty—The* **Fugitive** *Slaves* shows an enslaved family fleeing the South on horseback for freedom in the North.

Female Spy

Belle Boyd was a Confederate spy during the Civil War. She once listened in to the conversations of Union soldiers in a hotel room, hiding in a closet in the room and spying on them through a knothole in a door that she had secretly enlarged.

Belle rode through the night to give the information she had gathered from Union soldiers to the Confederate army.

Helping the War Effort

Women were not allowed to join either the Union or Confederate armies. However, many women felt it was their duty to help in any way they could to support the war effort. One way they could do that was by volunteering as nurses on the battlefield and in hospitals. With thousands of men killed and wounded, and few doctors available, much of the care for injured soldiers fell to these brave women.

Wartime Medicine

Medical care at the time of the war was very different from what it is today. There were no antibiotics to treat **infections**. Doctors were only just beginning to understand the existence of germs, and the critical importance of maintaining clean and sanitary conditions to avoid infection.

Dr Mary Edwards Walker was the only female surgeon to serve in battle during the Civil War and the only woman to ever have been awarded the Congressional Medal of Honor.

Women and the Wounded

Thousands of women, many from the North, volunteered to become nurses. They dressed wounds and assisted doctors with surgeries, including **amputations**. They spent time with the wounded, cheering their spirits, praying with them, and even helping them write letters home to their families. One of the most famous nurses of the war was Clara Barton, who was often called the "Angel of the Battlefield."

After the war, Clara Barton founded the American Red Cross.

WITNESS TO WAR

One nurse, Ella Wolcott, wrote about the work of women in hospitals during the Civil War and the vital role they performed:

"I have been a 'female nurse' since a year ago last October and only regret that I did not go in the beginning when a mistaken **humility** is all that withheld me ... I went in with many misgivings—but now I KNOW what women are worth in the hospitals. It is no light thing to hear a man say he owes you his life and then to know that mother, wife, sister, or child bless you in their prayers."

Humility means to be humble and modest.

Ella writes about "mistaken humility." What do you think she means by this?

What do you think Ella gained through her experience of nursing soldiers?

Deadly Diseases

Of the estimated more than 600,000 men who died during the Civil War, about two-thirds of them did not die directly from enemy fire, but from infections and diseases, such as tuberculosis, dysentery, measles, and typhoid fever. Disease spread quickly through war camps because of the dirty conditions and poor **sanitation** that existed there.

Hospital Horror

When injured soldiers were taken to makeshift hospitals, they did not fare much better than in the camps. Early in the war, hospitals had little organization. They were crowded, with more wounded men than they could handle. A hospital might be nothing more than tents outside, with wounded men lying everywhere, just on blankets on the ground.

Playing Their Part

The women who left home to become Civil War nurses were generally unmarried, educated, and from middle-class families. Not all women were able to leave home to play their part to support the war but, throughout the North and South, women found many other ways to contribute to the war effort.

Women Together

One of the most important services that women could offer was to help provide essential supplies. These could include anything from blankets and socks to bandages and food. Amid the uncertainty of wartime, many women channeled their energies into collecting food or medical supplies for the soldiers. Making clothes for their husbands, sons, and brothers also gave them a sense of purpose. Coming together at events such as local sewing bees had a further benefit—women were able to connect with others who were suffering the same hardships and anxieties that they were.

An Army of Volunteers

Some women extended their relief efforts and worked with organizations such as the United States Sanitary Commission, which operated across the North. The agency was created to support sick and wounded soldiers, and to promote clean and healthy conditions in Union army camps. Thousands of volunteers, many of whom were women, ran kitchens in army camps, oversaw soldiers' homes, and sewed uniforms.

Changing the Face of Nursing During Warfare

Before the war, Dorothea Dix had spent time overseas finding out how people with mental ill health were treated. After returning to America, and with the outbreak of war, she became a nurse for the Union army. Dorothea was placed in charge of nurses for the army, and given the job of recruiting them. She set very high standards, and often recruited plain-looking, older women, whom she believed would make better nurses and be less distracting to soldiers in army camps! She soon became known for advancing nursing in wartime, and treating injured Confederate and Union soldiers alike.

During her time with the Union army, Dorothea Dix recruited more than 3,000 nurses.

Women Fighters

Not all women were content to support the war effort from the sidelines. Though women were not allowed to join either the Union or Confederate armies, there are hundreds of known cases where women posed as men to join the army. Some, such as Lizzie Compton, were discovered by doctors after being wounded in battle. Others, such as Jennie Hodgers, went through the war without being found out. Some were only discovered when their babies were born in army camps! Like Belle Boyd, some women spied. Pauline Cushman was a famous Union spy.

Pauline Cushman was captured by the Confederates and sentenced to hang to death. However, she was rescued just three days before her execution.

Rose O'Neal Greenhow, shown left with her daughter, was another Confederate spy. She lost her life to the cause, smuggling gold through a Union blockade in 1864.

CHAPTER 4

THE CHILDREN WHO WITNESSED WAR

Women were not the only ones affected by a changed home life during the Civil War. Millions of children said goodbye to their fathers and older brothers, knowing they might never see them again. Families worked hard to stay as connected as they could to the soldiers who had left to fight. Writing letters was one way to keep in touch.

Some families even visited their loved ones in army camps, and stayed with them!

Letters That Tell Stories

Today, we can keep in touch with friends and family in many ways, including via telephone calls, texts, emails, and video chats. During the Civil War, none of this technology existed. The only way for families to communicate with soldiers in distant camps was by writing letters. The letters written to soldiers often told of daily life at home. Families also discussed major events of the war. The letters that soldiers wrote back describe battles and army life.

Not Forgotten

Families were happy to receive letters from relatives and friends in the armies, and to know they were still alive and well. Soldiers were equally anxious to receive letters that showed their loved ones were thinking of them, and that they had not been forgotten.

PRIMARY SOURCE

Losing Their Homes

The photo below was taken in 1862. It shows an American family on the move during the Civil War. The war brought hardship and displacement for many families, forcing them to leave their homes. What do you think it would have been like for children who experienced this? How may it have affected them?

Lessons from the Past

As important as letters from family were for people at the time of the Civil War, they are important for us today, too. The letters that have survived give us a glimpse of what life was like during the war, what people thought about major events, and what they believed they were fighting for. They are an invaluable source of information.

Before the War

In the years before the Civil War, families often had many children. The more children there were in a family, the more hands there were to help. Life was busy and there was a lot of work to do, so a large family helped spread the workload. A large family was especially important for families who farmed. Both parents and children generally woke before the Sun was up and got to work. Children did many tasks—they milked cows, gathered eggs from the henhouse, and fetched the day's water from the well.

Boys and Girls

Older sons often helped their father plow fields, while daughters often helped their mother prepare food for the day and wash clothes. Many children also went to school, while others studied at home. Along with working hard and studying, children made time for play. They enjoyed fishing, hunting, and having fun with siblings and friends, just like children today. Although daily life had its challenges, it was a world away from what was to come years later when Civil War broke out.

WITNESS TO WAR

Tillie Pierce lived in Gettysburg and was a teenage girl in 1863 when Confederate soldiers were ordered to raid the town for supplies. This is an extract from her account:

"What a horrible sight! There they were, human beings! Clad almost in rags, covered with dust, riding wildly, pell-mell down the hill toward our home! Shouting, yelling most unearthly, cursing, brandishing their revolvers, and firing right and left. I was fully persuaded that the Rebels had actually come at last. What they would do with us was a fearful question to my young mind."

What effect do you think the sight of enemy soldiers firing right and left may have had on Tillie?

What do you think she means by "What they would do with us was a fearful question to my young mind."?

A Tough New World

Before the Civil War, life for many families was difficult. When the war began, however, conditions for many families became even harder. With their fathers and older brothers away fighting, children often took on new responsibilities as their families learned to adjust to life during war. Children helped their mothers run farms, performing difficult tasks such as harvesting crops and butchering animals. Many took care of younger siblings while their mothers worked.

Learning Loyalty

Some children had to leave school so they could provide more help at home. For those who were lucky enough to stay in school, lessons often focused on the war, promoting one or the other side's cause, and encouraging only absolute loyalty. Children were taught that the war was justified and that they should support whatever side their state supported. It was an education in warfare and **patriotism**.

The formal teaching of Black children only began at the end of the Civil War. Before then, these children mostly worked to support their families.

Survival in the South

Many Northerners faced hardships during the Civil War, such as separation from their husbands, sons, and brothers, and not knowing if their loved ones would ever return. However, Southerners suffered all this and then some. For them, every aspect of life was affected by war, as many of the deadly and desperate battles were taking place in their own backyards!

A Southern Battleground

Most of the battles of the Civil War took place in the South. This meant that Southern families—more often than those in the North—were direct witnesses to the harsh realities of war. Many towns and cities in the South were destroyed, including Atlanta, Georgia. Some parts of Atlanta were destroyed by Confederate troops as they **retreated**, though most of the destruction was at the hands of occupying Union troops led by General William T. Sherman. When Sherman's troops had left, out of 3,600 homes and buildings around the city center, only 400 were still standing.

Southern Starvation

As the war went on, the North was able to block many supplies from moving through the South. This meant that items families needed, including food, became either very expensive or impossible to find. Confederate money became worthless, which made it even harder for families to buy the things they needed to survive. Many Southern families were close to starvation. What few food supplies and valuables they did have were often stolen by bands of Union—or even Confederate—troops, who were also hungry. Some families were forced to leave their homes.

This illustration shows Confederate soldiers driving enslaved people south in a desperate attempt to stop them escaping.

WITNESS TO WAR

A woman in the town of Richmond witnessed firsthand the terrible starvation that took place in the South. This is a scene she described in a letter she wrote to a friend in 1863:

"I sat on a bench near, and one of the number ... took the seat beside me. She was a pale, emaciated girl, not more than eighteen ... As she raised her hand to remove her sunbonnet ... revealed the mere skeleton of an arm ... 'That's all that's left of me' she said ... We are starving."

Emaciated means very thin.

What effect do you think having so little food had on Southerners and their attitude toward the Civil War?

Enslaved people who did manage to escape the South often fled from their owners to Union army camps.

Joining the Fight

Throughout the war, children were encouraged to support their soldiers in any way they could. For most, this meant raising money and collecting supplies. Some children took their support a step further, though, and joined the fight themselves.

Boy Soldiers

The Union army set the minimum age for soldiers at 18 years old. However, it is thought that around 100,000 Union soldiers were boys under the age of 15. The Confederate army did not set an age requirement. Of the total number of Civil War soldiers, it is thought that about 20 percent were under the age of 15. Young boys were generally able to join the Union and Confederate armies by lying about their age. As the war went on, the armies became increasingly desperate for more soldiers. Recruiters—people who looked for new soldiers—often accepted boys into the army even if they suspected they were underage.

Other Roles

Boys also joined the army in other roles—as musicians, drummer boys, messengers, and scouts. These were roles that should have kept the boys safe for the most part. However, in the middle of a battle, many boys found they had to fight to protect both themselves and their fellow soldiers.

These children are watching soldiers prepare to go into the first full-scale battle of the Civil War—Bull Run.

A Child Hero

One of the most famous child soldiers of the war was a boy named Johnny Clem. He was only 10 years old when he joined the Union army as a drummer boy. At the Battle of Chickamauga, when a Confederate colonel demanded that Johnny surrender, or give up, the boy, then 12, raised his musket and shot the officer. Johnny Clem became a hero, and continued to serve in the US army until he retired in 1915.

Johnny Clem, shown right, wore his Union army uniform proudly.

"I want to say, as we lay there and the shells were flying over us, my thoughts went back to my home, and I thought what a foolish boy I was to run away and get into such a mess as I was in. I would have been glad to have seen my father coming after me."

WITNESS TO WAR

The words shown left were written by a boy named Elisha Stockwell, who was 15 years old when he joined the Union army:

Many boys joined the fighting because they thought it would be a great adventure. What do you think it was like for these boys when they experienced the reality of war, with all its horrors?

CHAPTER 5

THE END OF THE WAR

After four long years of fighting, Confederate troops were worn down and spread thin. Northern resources had held out, while Southern resources had been heavily depleted. Hundreds of thousands of men on both sides of the conflict had been killed, and many more were injured. The fighting was nearly over, and though the Confederacy had won many of the war's battles, the Union would win the war itself.

A Turning Point

On April 9, 1865, one of the last battles of the Civil War was fought in Virginia. Following the Union army's Siege of Petersburg, which had lasted for 10 months, General Robert E. Lee and the army of Northern Virginia left the Confederate capital of Richmond. Lee hoped to move his soldiers back to North Carolina and meet up with other Confederate troops. However, Union forces cut off their retreat at the Appomattox Court House. The Confederate forces tried to break through, but they were surrounded. Lee sent a message to Union army commander Ulysses S. Grant that he would like to meet to discuss surrender.

The Moment of Surrender

On the afternoon of April 9, Lee officially surrendered to Grant. Within two months, nearly all Confederate troops had surrendered.

This image shows General Lee surrendering to Union General Ulysses S. Grant at Appomattox Court House in Virginia on April 9, 1865.

WITNESS TO WAR

Caroline Cowles Richards was a young woman who lived in New York during the Civil War. She kept a diary, and recorded hearing of the war's end:

"Whether I am in the body, or out of the body, I know not, but one thing I know, Lee has surrendered! And all the people seem crazy in consequence. The bells are ringing, boys and girls, men and women are running through the streets wild with excitement; the flags are all flying, one from the top of our church, and such a 'hurrah boys' generally, I never dreamed of."

Why do you think Caroline said she did not know if she was "in the body, or out of the body"?

What does Caroline's account tell us about people's emotions on hearing of the end of the war?

Caroline's high spirits, like those of many other Unionists, were shattered shortly after the end of the war by the news that President Lincoln had been shot ...

The Death of Lincoln

Just a few days after the end of the war, on April 14, President Abraham Lincoln was shot while attending a play in Washington, D.C. He would die early the next day. When an important person, such as a president, is killed it is called an assassination. The man who assassinated Abraham Lincoln was an actor named John Wilkes Booth. By killing the president, he and his conspirators hoped to revive the Confederacy. Booth was cornered and killed during capture on April 26. Vice President Andrew Johnson was sworn in as US president on April 15.

An End to Suffering?

With the war over, there was hope that family life might go back to the way it had been before the fighting began. However, hundreds of thousands of men never went home. Women had become widows and children had lost their fathers. Tragically, one out of every three households in the South had lost at least one family member.

Families had to rebuild their shattered lives in towns and cities that had also been scarred.

More Than Physical

For soldiers, the aftereffects were not only physical. Many also suffered emotional and psychological problems on returning home. They often found it difficult to adjust to their life at home after years on the battlefield and the horrors that they had seen. Psychological problems were not well understood at the time, and there was very little help available to those who were suffering.

These Black soldiers are returning to their families at the end of the war. Although the relief of reuniting with their loved ones must have been huge, many relived the trauma of their war experience for years to come.

Returning Home

Many army companies had been recruited from small towns and counties close together. When these companies were wiped out on the battlefield, it was devastating for their hometowns. Some towns and counties had lost almost their entire male population. It was extremely difficult for their families and other remaining townspeople to continue with their lives after such an enormous loss.

Living with the War

Of the soldiers who did return home, many lived with the effects of the war for the rest of their days. Large numbers of men had lost one or more limbs to amputation, or cutting off, to save their lives. This loss of limbs made manual labor almost impossible for many. With the consequent loss of labor and income, many families fell into poverty and terrible hardship was endured despite the end of the war.

Do Not Forget

During the four years of fighting, there was not often a lot of time to reflect on what had been lost. People were more concerned with everyday survival and the safety of their loved ones. However, once the war was over, many in the North and South worked to heal the country's wounds and to make sure that future generations would not forget their struggles.

Terrible Losses

By the war's end, hundreds of thousands of men had died. That was between two and three percent of the entire US population at the time. In some of the major battles, thousands had died in a single day. In the middle of war, there was little time or manpower to deal with the huge number of bodies.

This is a memorial to the Massachusetts 54th, an all-Black unit in the Civil War. It stands near the Massachusetts State House in Boston.

The Arlington National Cemetery, in Virginia, marks the many lives lost due to the Civil War.

A National Need

Before the war, there were no national cemeteries. There were no procedures in place for identifying bodies, burying them, or notifying family members. The Civil War made Americans aware that these things were very much needed. Arlington National Cemetery, the most famous American national cemetery today, was established in 1864. In 1867, two years after the end of fighting, Congress set up a program to rebury Union soldiers in 74 national cemeteries. The exclusion of Confederate soldiers upset many in the South, adding to their trauma.

Remembering the Dead

With thousands of the war's soldiers buried, families began gathering at graves and bringing flowers. This occasion was known as Decoration Day. In 1868, a former Union general named John Logan officially declared May 30 as a day to decorate the graves of fallen soldiers. Today, we celebrate this important event as Memorial Day, on the last Monday in May. The day is used to mark and remember the deaths of the thousands of soldiers of the Civil War and all deaths of US soldiers in conflicts since.

CHAPTER 6

AFTER THE WAR

With the Civil War over, the question facing the US government was how to reconcile the two sides of the conflict and bring the former Confederate states back into the Union. The time period beginning with the end of the war in 1865 and lasting until 1877 is known as the Reconstruction Era. During this time, the US government tried to "reconstruct" the South.

Union for All

Abraham Lincoln believed it would be best to bring the South back into the Union quickly and with as little conflict as possible. After Lincoln's assassination, President Andrew Johnson supported this plan. However, there were others in the government who believed that former Confederates should be punished for their rebellion. This group, called the "Radical Republicans," also wanted to give Black people equal rights, including the right to vote in elections. The forceful group and President Johnson could not find an agreement.

Change and Anger

However, the next president, Ulysses S. Grant, sided with the Radical Republicans. Congress removed many state governments in the South and put the US army in charge. New elections were held in

Ulysses S. Grant was president between 1869 and 1877, during the postwar period that became known as the Reconstruction Era.

Many celebrated the liberation of Black people, but there were many white Southerners who were angered by the change.

which Black people were allowed to vote and many former Confederate leaders were not. The policies angered many Southerners. A group called the Klu Klux Klan began to carry out attacks against Black people and white people who supported Reconstruction. Often through voter fraud and violence, groups of white Democrats took back state governments one by one.

Agreeing to Compromise

After a controversial election in 1876, the Electoral Commission agreed to declare Republican Rutherford B. Hayes as the next president over Democrat Samuel Tilden. In exchange, Hayes was compelled to remove the last of the US troops in former Confederate states. This so-called Compromise of 1877 effectively ended Reconstruction.

WITNESS TO WAR

There was real fear and anger among many Southerners after defeat, and concern about the changes to their way of life. Some are expressed in this extract from a diary kept by a plantation owner named Henry William Ravenel:

"The experiment is now to be tried. The Negro is not only to be emancipated but is to become a citizen with all the rights and privileges! It produced a financial, political, and social revolution at the South, fearful to contemplate its ultimate effects."

Emancipated means freed.

Why do you think some Southerners were so fearful of former enslaved people having rights?

Failures and Successes

The Reconstruction Era is considered to be mostly a failure. Many of the actions of the US government in the South caused even more anger and resentment. However, some good came from the era in the form of the Reconstruction **amendments**—three amendments to the **US Constitution** relating to the rights and treatment of Black people.

Constitution Changes

The US government is designed so that laws and rules written into the Constitution are the most important, overruling those passed by the states. States cannot pass laws that go against the laws of the US Constitution. Therefore, the best way to enact a controversial law, such as the banning of slavery, was to make it an amendment, or change, to the Constitution. The former Confederate states were then forced to ratify, or approve, these amendments as a condition of once again having representation in the federal government.

Despite serving in the Union army and fighting for freedom, the rights of Black soldiers such as Nicholas Biddle were not recognized fully until the passing of the Fifteenth Amendment (see opposite).

PRIMARY SOURCE

A Hard Road to Travel

These are the words sung by Black soldiers who fought for the Union army. They tell of the struggle both of the war and also for freedom from slavery.

> *"So, rally, boys, rally, let us never mind the past;*
> *We had a hard road to travel, but our day is coming fast,*
> *For God is for the right, and we have no need to fear,*
> *The Union must be saved by the colored volunteer."*

Moves Toward Equality

The Thirteenth Amendment, ratified on December 6, 1865, abolished slavery within the United States. The Fourteenth Amendment gave citizenship to all people born or naturalized in the United States, including former enslaved people, and was ratified on July 9, 1868. Declaring Black citizens was an important step. In the 1857 Dred Scott case, the Supreme Court had ruled that neither free nor enslaved Black people were citizens, and therefore had no right to sue for their freedom in federal court. The Fourteenth Amendment gave them that right.

The Right to Vote

The Fifteenth Amendment—stating that the right of male citizens to vote could not be denied because of race or color—was the last of the Reconstruction amendments, ratified on February 3, 1870. All three Reconstruction amendments advanced equality but did not solve the problems of racial injustice.

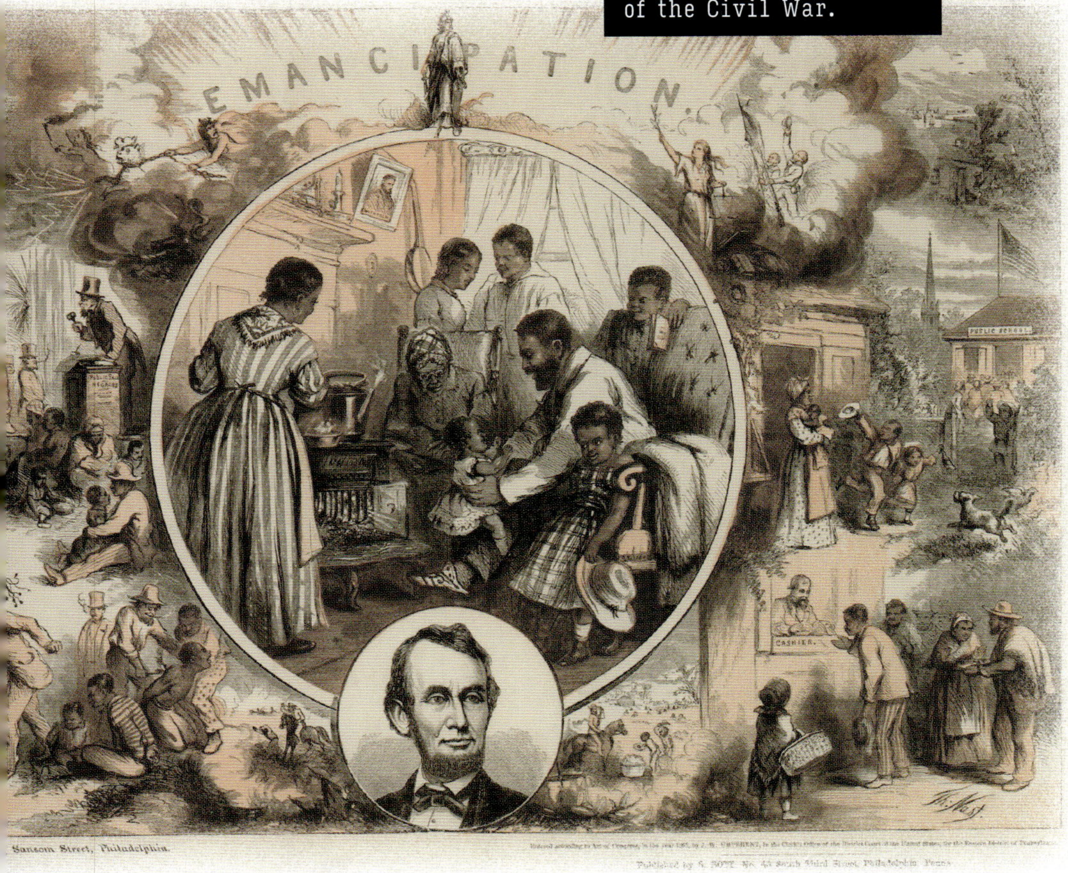

This print was created in 1865 to celebrate the end of slavery and of the Civil War.

Fighting Against Equality

After the Reconstruction Era, Southern Democrats took control of the state governments of the former Confederate states. While they could not pass laws that went against the US Constitution, they found many ways around the laws. The rules that kept people segregated by race and unequal for nearly 100 years are often known as the Jim Crow laws.

Voting Confusion

During Reconstruction, for a short time, Black males had the right to vote in elections. However, once Southern Democrats regained control of state governments, they introduced laws that effectively prevented Blacks from voting. For example, literacy tests required Black people to answer difficult—and sometimes nonsensical—questions before being allowed to vote, which most people could not do. Poll taxes compelled people to pay a certain amount before being allowed to vote, which many poor people could not afford. Those who could not vote were also not allowed to serve on juries or hold public office, or positions of authority.

Rules of Separation

Black children and families also suffered because of Jim Crow laws. Most areas of daily life, such as public schools, libraries, workplaces, restaurants, restrooms, and even drinking fountains, were segregated. This meant that Black people and white people had to use separate facilities. Under the law, the facilities were supposed to be "separate but equal." However, schools and other facilities for Black people were underfunded and of lower quality.

Acts of violence against Black people continued to be perpetrated long after the end of the Civil War.

PRIMARY SOURCE

A Congress First

This 1872 image shows the first Black legislators in the history of the United States Congress. They are Robert C. De Large, Jefferson H. Long, H.R. Revels, Benj. S. Turner, Josiah T. Walls, Joseph H. Rainy, and R. Brown Elliot. How do you think the men in this image felt about becoming members of Congress? What effect do you think their appointment had on Southerners who were still opposed to equality?

The Civil Rights Movement

In the 1950s and 1960s, many people set out to change the culture of segregation and inequality for Black people. Using nonviolent protests and civil disobedience, heroes of the movement—such as Rosa Parks and Martin Luther King, Jr.—put their lives and freedom on the line to effect change. The Civil Rights Act of 1964, signed by President Lyndon Johnson, made it illegal to discriminate against a person based on their race, color, sex, national origin, or religion. The act finally ended the segregation of public schools and public places, and any practices used to prevent people from voting. It was a landmark moment.

Difficult to Forget

The Civil War was a hugely destructive conflict that claimed thousands of lives. Today, the conflict is often remembered through reenactments.

This image shows a reenactment of the 1863 Battle of Gettysburg.

The Legacy of War

The American Civil War remains the bloodiest war in US history. It had a huge influence over the country that we are today. We often focus on the soldiers who fought and died. However, it is important to remember that the war changed the lives of women, children, and families, both white and Black, free and enslaved, as well as the soldiers who fought.

Hardships and Horrors

The Civil War had a dramatic and lasting effect on our country. It took a long time to heal from the wounds and the hardship that the war inflicted, and some of that healing continues in the generations that came after. For those who lived through the Civil War, life would never be the same. On both sides of the conflict, nearly every person suffered loss. Hundreds of thousands lost a husband, brother, father, or son. Many families lost their homes and all of their possessions, too.

Hard-Won Victories

For all the loss, however, much was gained as well. Slavery was abolished, and the North and South slowly came back together to form a stronger country—more united than ever. Throughout the twentieth century, Black people made great gains in civil rights and equality. Once barred from voting, Black citizens now serve in key government positions.

Witness to the Past

The terrible losses and hardships of those who lived through the Civil War are remembered to this day, and their accounts as witnesses to history will shine a light on the horror of war forever. By remembering their stories, we can learn lessons about past conflicts and use those lessons to help us strive for a more peaceful future.

The huge loss of life and devastation caused by the war are remembered in Civil War monuments in Washington, D.C.

A TIMELINE FOR WAR

This timeline charts the key events of the Civil War.

1850

September 18: The Fugitive Slave Act is passed by Congress, requiring all escaped enslaved people to be returned to their owners, even if they had reached free states. The law also required citizens in free states to cooperate.

1854

May 30: The Kansas-Nebraska Act, allowing settlers in new territories to vote freely on the slavery issue, is signed into law.

1860

November 6: Abraham Lincoln is elected president of the United States.

December 20: South Carolina officially secedes from the Union—within three months, six more states will secede.

1861

January 29: Kansas is admitted to the United States as a free state.

February 8–9: The Confederate States of America is formed. Jefferson Davis is elected to serve as president.

March 4: Abraham Lincoln is inaugurated (formally confirmed) as US president.

April 15: President Lincoln calls for 75,000 volunteers to enlist in the Union army for three months.

April 17: The state of Virginia votes to secede from the Union—the eighth state to do so.

May 24: The Union army captures Alexandria, Virginia.

July 21: The First Battle of Bull Run, the first major battle of the war, is a victory for the Confederates.

1862

February 6: The Union army captures Fort Henry, Tennessee, opening the state for a Union advance.

March 8–9: The Battle of the Ironclads, in which the Confederate USS *Virginia* destroys two of the Union's wooden ships and fights to a draw with the Union's ironclad, the USS *Monitor*.

April 6–7: The Battle of Shiloh is fought. It is a Union victory, though both sides suffer huge losses.

August 28–30: The Second Battle of Bull Run, also named the Second Battle of Manassas, is fought, resulting in a Confederate victory.

September 17: The Battle of Antietam is fought. The inconclusive battle is the first to take place in Union territory. It remains the bloodiest single-day battle in US history.

December 11–15: The Battle of Fredericksburg is a Confederate victory with heavy Union losses.

1863

January 1: Abraham Lincoln issues the **Emancipation Proclamation**, freeing enslaved people in Southern territories.

July 1–3: The Battle of Gettysburg is fought, with the largest number of casualties of any Civil War battle. It is a Union victory.

July 13–16: Riots to protest the draft are held in New York City.

November 19: Abraham Lincoln delivers a speech called the Gettysburg Address, about the principles of equality, to inspire and unite the nation.

1864

June 28: Abraham Lincoln repeals the fugitive slave laws.

September 2: Union commander General William T. Sherman captures the city of Atlanta.

November 8: Abraham Lincoln is reelected as US president.

1865

January 31: The US Congress passes the Thirteenth Amendment, abolishing slavery.

April 9: Robert E. Lee, commander of the Confederate army of Northern Virginia, surrenders (gives up) to Union commander Ulysses S. Grant.

April 14: Abraham Lincoln is shot by John Wilkes Booth in Washington, D.C. He dies the next day.

June 2: The Confederate port of Galveston, Texas, finally surrenders, ending the war.

June 19: Enslaved people in Texas are finally informed of the end of the war.

GLOSSARY

abolitionists people who support the abolition (the stopping) of a practice, such as slavery

agriculture the science or practice of growing crops and raising livestock

amendments additions or changes to a document, law, or set of laws, such as the Constitution

amputations surgical operations to cut off or remove limbs or parts of limbs

artillery cannons, large guns, or other weapons for firing over long distances

bayonets sharp knives attached to the front ends of rifles for use in close-range combat

casualties people who are injured or killed in an accident or a war

citizen a person who is born in a country or legally permitted to live there and benefit from its rights and protection

compromise a way of avoiding conflict by giving up something in order to reach agreement

economy the wealth and resources of a country or region in terms of goods and services

Emancipation Proclamation an official order, signed by Abraham Lincoln during the Civil War, which freed all enslaved people in the South

fugitive someone who is running away from someone or something

infections illnesses caused by germs

ironclad ships ships covered with iron or steel to protect them in battle

muskets long-barreled firearms used before the invention of more efficient rifles

patriotism pride in one's country

political party an organized group sharing similar beliefs about how a country should be run

representatives people elected to act or speak for the group who have chosen them

resources supplies of something necessary or valuable that can be used when required

retreated backed away from a fight or a dangerous, unpleasant, or difficult situation

sanitation use of measures, such as cleanliness, to prevent disease and protect public health

secede to withdraw from a group or a country

telegraph a machine used to send messages through wires using coded signals

US Constitution a document adopted in 1788 that explains the different parts of the US government and the basic rights of citizens

FIND OUT MORE

Books

Captivating History. *American History for Kids: A Captivating Guide to Major Events in US History* (History for Children). Captivating History, 2023.

DK. *American Civil War* (DK Eyewitness). DK Children, 2023.

Smith, Elliot. *Hidden Heroes in the Civil War* (Alternator Books). Lerner Publishing Group, 2023.

Websites

Learn about Arlington Cemetery, its monuments, and notable graves at:
www.arlingtoncemetery.mil

Find out more about the Civil War at:
https://kids.britannica.com/students/article/American-Civil-War/273689

Discover when and where Civil War battles were fought at:
storymaps.esri.com/stories/civilwar

Publisher's note to educators and parents:
All the websites featured above have been carefully reviewed to ensure that they are suitable for students. However, many websites change often, and we cannot guarantee that a site's future contents will continue to meet our high standards of educational value. Please be advised that students should be closely monitored whenever they access the Internet.

INDEX

About the Author

Kelly Roberts has written many history books for young people. In researching the eyewitness accounts in this book, she has learned more about the human experience of war and the devastation it caused for those who witnessed it.